Dear Parents,

Welcome to the Scholastic Reader series. We have taken over 80 years of experience with teachers, parents, and children and put it into a program that is designed to match your child's interests and skills.

Level 1—Short sentences and stories made up of words kids can sound out using their phonics skills and words that are important to remember.

Level 2—Longer sentences and stories with words kids need to know and new "big" words that they will want to know.

Level 3—From sentences to paragraphs to longer stories, these books have large "chunks" of texts and are made up of a rich vocabulary.

Level 4—First chapter books with more words and fewer pictures.

It is important that children learn to read well enough to succeed in school and beyond. Here are ideas for reading this book with your child:

- Look at the book together. Encourage your child to read the title and make a prediction about the story.
- Read the book together. Encourage your child to sound out words when appropriate. When your child struggles, you can help by providing the word.
- Encourage your child to retell the story. This is a great way to check for comprehension.
- Have your child take the fluency test on the last page to check progress.

Scholastic Readers are designed to support your child's efforts to learn how to read at every age and every stage. Enjoy helping your child learn to read and love to read.

—**Francie Alexander**
Chief Education Officer
Scholastic Education

PHOTO CREDITS

Pages 4, 8, 11, 19, 23: Schomburg Center for Research in Black Culture,
New York Public Library
Pages 13, 14, 21: Corbis
Page 24: courtesy Third World Press
Page 32: Virginia Hamilton portrait © by Ron Rovtar
Page 37 left: courtesy Virginia Hamilton; 37 right: *Zeely* paperback edition from
Aladdin Books/Macmillan Publishing Company, cover illustration © by Jerry Pinkney
Pages 38, 47: Scholastic, Inc.
Page 39: courtesy Virginia Hamilton
Pages 40, 42, 45 left: courtesy Walter Dean Myers; 45 right: *Fallen Angels*, Scholastic Inc.

Text copyright © 2001 by Lynda Jones.
Illustrations copyright © 2001 by Ron Garnett.
Activities copyright © 2004 Scholastic Inc.
All rights reserved. Published by Scholastic Inc.
SCHOLASTIC, CARTWHEEL BOOKS, and associated logos
are trademarks and/or registered trademarks of Scholastic Inc.

"My People": from *The Collected Poems of Langston Hughes*.
Copyright © 1994 by the Estate of Langston Hughes.
Reprinted by permission of Alfred A Knopf, a division of Random House, Inc.

Library of Congress Cataloging-in-Publication Data is available.

ISBN: 0-590-48035-9

10 9 8   06   07   08
                    Printed in the U.S.A. 23 • First printing, January 2001

**Produced by
Just Us Books, Inc.**
356 Glenwood Avenue
East Orange, NJ 07017

GREAT BLACK HEROES

Five Famous Writers

by **Lynda Jones**

Illustrated by **Ron Garnett**

Scholastic Reader — Level 4

SCHOLASTIC INC.

New York Toronto London Auckland Sydney
Mexico City New Delhi Hong Kong Buenos Aires

James Langston Hughes
BORN 1902 - DIED 1967

The Dream Keeper

James Langston Hughes was born on February 1, 1902, in Joplin, Missouri. He was named after his father, James Nathaniel Hughes, and his mother, Carrie Langston. Everyone called the boy Langston.

Shortly after Langston was born, his father moved to Mexico. Five years later, Langston, his mother, and Grandma Langston joined his father. But soon after the three arrived, an earthquake shook Mexico. Frightened, they returned to the United States the next day. Langston didn't see his father again for 11 years.

Carrie Hughes had to travel far away to get to her job, so Langston lived with his grandmother in Lawrence, Kansas. Grandma Langston read him many stories. Langston loved to read, too. Years later, he said, "I learned to love books more than people."

When Langston was in the eighth grade, he was elected class poet. His teacher asked him to write a poem for his graduating class. This was Langston's first poem. When he read it on graduation day, everyone clapped. In high school, he wrote poetry for the school magazine. Langston hoped the world would one day read his work.

Langston's father invited him to Mexico again when he was 17. On the train ride to Toluca, Mexico, the boy looked at the muddy Mississippi River. Its color reminded him of Black people. He wrote a poem called "The Negro Speaks of Rivers."

Langston loved to hear his grandmother read out loud and tell stories about his family's history.

Langston attended Columbia University in New York City and later became a student at Lincoln University in Pennsylvania.

The poem was printed in *Crisis,* one of the first Black publications in America. Many people now read Langston's poetry for the first time.

The young writer grew even more excited about writing. But Langston's father had not wanted his son to become a writer. He did not believe Langston would make any money, but he gave in after he saw his son's poems in the magazine. He felt proud of Langston when the young man chose to go to New York City and attend Columbia University.

In New York, Langston discovered the beauty of Harlem, a mostly Black community. He loved being around his people. From then on, Langston wrote more poems and stories about them.

Langston worked hard, but he didn't like school. He left and found work as a mess boy on a ship, the *West Hesseltine*, which sailed to Africa. The beauty of the land and people amazed him. He praised Africa in "My People."

The night is beautiful,
So the faces of my people.

The stars are beautiful,
So the eyes of my people.

Beautiful, also, is the sun.
Beautiful, also, are the souls
of my people.

The Africans, however, made fun of Langston. They said his skin wasn't brown enough. This made Langston sad.

Langston left Africa and continued to travel around the world. He worked at many different jobs. He was a guard, an assistant cook, and a painter. Langston wrote poems in his spare time. Some were published in Black magazines, such as *Opportunity* and *Crisis*. Langston was greeted warmly on his return to Harlem. His work had become well known by many writers.

When Langston turned 23, he wanted to go back to college, but he needed money. Soon he met Charlotte Mason, a wealthy woman who loved his poems. Charlotte Mason paid for young Langston's schooling. He called her "Godmother."

In 1926, Langston enrolled in Lincoln University, an all-Black school near Philadelphia, Pennsylvania. A year later he published his first novel, *Not Without Laughter*, a fictional story about his life. The book won the Harmon Gold Award that year for the best Black literature. Langston received $400 in prize money.

At Lincoln, Langston published many poems and stories and essays. *The New York Times* newspaper called him a "poet with promise."

After Langston graduated from college in 1929, he wrote two children's books. *The*

A year after his first book was published, Langston and his friends Jessie Fauset (left) and Zora Neale Hurston (right) visited Tuskegee Institute in Alabama.

Dream Keeper was a book of poems, and *Popo and Fifina,* published in 1932, was a storybook written with Arna Bontemps. It was based on a trip he had made to Haiti.

People enjoyed listening to Langston's poetry, but they weren't buying his books. The writer struggled to earn a living. He traveled around the country trying to sell his books and writing for magazines and news organizations such as the Associated Negro Press. It was the oldest and largest Black press service. The Press supplied news stories concerning Blacks to Black newspapers nationwide.

In 1937, Langston went to Spain to write articles about the Spanish Civil War for the Press. Later, he wrote news stories about Black soldiers who served in World War II. By 1945, Langston had his own column in the *Chicago Defender*, the most respected Black newspaper in the country. He wrote about Black life and race relations.

Even though Langston was known as a poet, he also wrote plays, novels, and biographies. He encouraged Black writers such as James Baldwin and Gwendolyn Brooks. He met important Black leaders such as Martin Luther King, Jr.; W. E. B. DuBois; and educator Mary McLeod Bethune.

In 1960, the National Association for the Advancement of Colored People (NAACP) awarded Langston the Spingarn Medal for his inspiring work. A year later, Langston was inducted into the National Institute of Arts and Letters, which honors

Langston Hughes had many jobs before he became a full-time writer. Here, Langston works as a busboy at the Wardman Park Hotel in Washington, DC.

the accomplishments of Americans in literature and the arts.

President Lyndon B. Johnson awarded Langston another very great honor. In 1966, he made Langston the director of the First World Festival of Negro Arts in Dakar, Senegal. The festival was established by the president of Senegal, Leopold Sedar Senghor. Blacks from all over the world came together to share their culture with others of African descent.

Langston died on May 22, 1967, but his great works live on.

Richard Nathaniel Wright

BORN 1908 - DIED 1960

Native Son/Black Boy

Ella and Nathan Wright worked picking cotton on a plantation near Roxie, Mississippi. The Wrights lived in a small cabin on a run-down farm. Their son Richard Nathaniel Wright was born there on September 4, 1908.

Young Richard loved to play on the farm. He skipped between rows of planted vegetables, watched horses clop by, and, from a nearby river, caught crayfish in a tin can. Richard had fun. But that quickly changed.

In 1913, the family decided to move to find better jobs. The Wrights and their sons, Richard and two-year-old Leon, boarded the *Kate Adams* steamboat to Memphis, Tennessee. In Memphis, they rented two small rooms in someone's house. Richard's father, unable to find a job, left the family. He never came back. Then Richard's mother became ill and couldn't work. There was not enough food to eat. Many times, dry bread and tea were all they had to eat for the day.

The Wrights moved from state to state. They lived with one relative, then another. For a time, Richard lived with his grandmother in Jackson, Mississippi. Richard went to school, but by the time he turned 12 he had less than two full years of schooling. His mother taught him how to read. Reading helped Richard forget about being poor.

As a young boy, Richard enjoyed playing outdoors.

While he was in school, Richard also worked on his writing. One day in his eighth-grade class, Richard wrote a story called "The Voodoo of Hell's Half-Acre." The tale was about an evil man who tries to cheat a widow out of her home.

After school, Richard marched into the offices of the *Southern Register*, a Black newspaper. He showed his story to an editor. "This is quite a tale!" said the newsman, who decided to print it in the paper. This was Richard's first story, published in 1924.

After graduating from junior high school, Richard found a job in Memphis, Tennessee. He worked as an errand boy for an eyeglass shop. He read in his spare time.

In those days, Blacks weren't allowed to have library cards. A White coworker let Richard borrow his card. Richard wrote notes to the librarian that said he had permission to check out books. He pretended that his White coworker wrote the notes. Richard read everything he could get his hands on.

Like these Blacks, Richard Wright and his family were a part of the Great Northern Migration.

In 1927, when Richard was 19 years old, he moved to Chicago where he began his literary career. A number of his poems and short stories were published in journals and in newspapers. Then, in 1937, Richard packed his bags again—and his typewriter—and hitched a ride to New York City. New York City was the literary capital of America. There he worked at the *Daily Worker* newspaper.

One day Richard learned about a national writing contest in *Story Magazine.* He sent in four stories. To Richard's surprise, one of his stories, "Fire and Cloud," won. The prize was $500. Then someone offered to publish all of his stories! This became Richard's first book, published in 1938. It was called *Uncle Tom's Children: Four Novellas.* The book is about how *racism*, being mistreated by other races for being different, affected Mississippi Blacks.

Richard was so happy that he started working on his next book right away. In the mornings he went to a park near his home. He sat on a small hill and wrote for hours.

In 1940, his book *Native Son* was on bookshelves everywhere. The book was about how poverty and racism affected a young Black man. People everywhere, Black and White, read the book. Richard Wright was becoming famous.

A year later, the 33-year-old writer married a woman named Ellen Poplar. They had two daughters, Julia and Rachel. That same year, the National Association for the Advancement of Colored People (NAACP) gave Richard an award for writing *Native Son. Native Son* was the first book written by a Black American to be chosen as a Book-of-the-Month Club selection.

Richard Wright works at his desk in his home, 14 Rue Monsieur le Prince, located in the Latin Quarter of Paris, France.

Months later, a successful play based on the book appeared at the St. James Theatre in New York City. Ten years later, film makers would make the book into a movie.

In 1943, Richard began writing another powerful story. He wrote about growing up in the Deep South. The book, *Black Boy*, was published in 1945. It was an important book. It told of how Blacks couldn't eat in certain restaurants. In some places they had to go in the back door and not the front. Blacks had limited housing. They were treated badly based on skin color alone. Richard hoped that Whites would read the book, realize how unfair they had been to Blacks, and change.

Richard's book was a great success, but Whites still didn't treat him with respect. This made Richard so angry that the Wrights moved to Paris, France. There Richard and his family were respected. Richard wrote many books in his new homeland. He traveled all over Europe. He never returned to America.

*Richard Wright shakes hands in a 1948 meeting with
Gaston Monnerville, President of the Republic of France
and George Slocombe, President of the Press Group.*

In 1960, Richard had a heart attack and died. During his life, Richard Wright wrote 12 books. He gave speeches to many people all over the world about being poor and Black in America. But most of all, with his books, Richard Wright wanted to teach people that everyone should be treated equally.

Gwendolyn Elizabeth Brooks

BORN 1917

Poet Laureate

Gwendolyn Elizabeth Brooks was born on June 17, 1917, in Topeka, Kansas. Her mother was a schoolteacher. Her father was a janitor. After Gwendolyn's birth, the family moved to Chicago, Illinois.

Young Gwendolyn was quiet and shy. As she grew older, Gwendolyn learned to love words. Her nose was always stuck in a book. She could read two books a day! Gwendolyn especially loved poems by Paul Laurence Dunbar, a Black poet.

When she was only seven years old, Gwendolyn began writing rhymes and poems in a special notebook. Gwendolyn's mother encouraged her. "You're going to be the *lady* Paul Laurence Dunbar," exclaimed Mrs. Brooks.

Mrs. Brooks did Gwendolyn's chores so her daughter could spend more time writing. Gwendolyn's father gave her a desk. She loved reading and writing at her desk. She wrote about love, death, and nature. She wrote two or three poems a day.

One day Gwendolyn came across *Writer's Digest*, a magazine that listed publications where writers could send their work. She was very excited to discover that others were writing about their feelings, too. And they were getting published! Right away, Gwendolyn sent her poem "Eventide" to *American Childhood*, a children's magazine. Her poem was published in 1930. She was 13.

Gwendolyn kept writing in high school. She sent her poetry to professors and writers. They wrote back giving her advice. Then when Gwendolyn was 16, she

Gwendolyn loved to read and write at the desk her father gave her.

met the poet Langston Hughes at a poetry reading in church. She showed him her poems. Langston read them. Then he smiled and said, "These are good. You must continue to write." Gwendolyn later said, "He was an inspiration."

While still in high school, Gwendolyn wrote poems for the *Defender,* a Black Chicago newspaper. She kept to herself. She didn't go to school dances or sports games. Other children thought she was strange.

After high school, Gwendolyn attended Wilson Junior College, in Chicago, Illinois, and graduated in 1936. Two years later she met Henry Lowington Blakely II. He was a writer, too. They married and had two children, Henry and Nora.

Gwendolyn could never learn enough

Gwendolyn Brooks at the age of 14.

about poetry and poets. In 1941, she heard about a poetry workshop for young Black writers and joined the group. Writers shared their work with each other. Gwendolyn wrote poems about Black people and about what she heard or saw on the streets.

Gwendolyn received her first poetry award in 1943 from the Midwestern Writers' Conference. Her first book of poems, *A Street in Bronzeville*, was published two years later. The poems were about people who lived in her Chicago neighborhood.

In 1950, Gwendolyn Brooks received the highest honor—a Pulitzer Prize. Pulitzers are awarded to outstanding literary writers or journalists. Gwendolyn won the prize for *Annie Allen*, a book about the life of a young Black girl. Gwendolyn was the first Black writer to win the Pulitzer. She beamed with pride and joy.

Gwendolyn Brooks wrote many more books. In 1956, she wrote *Bronzeville Boys and Girls*, a poetry book for children that

Langston Hughes encouraged young Gwendolyn Brooks to write poetry. They supported each other's work. Here the two writers appear at Hall Branch Library in Chicago, 1949.

shows how they view the world. She traveled near and far, reading her poems to students and anyone else who would listen.

Gwendolyn wanted young people to love poetry, too. She taught poetry in schools in Illinois and New York. She gave poetry awards to talented young poets. She used her own money to pay for the awards.

In 1967, Gwendolyn attended a Black writers' conference at Fisk University in Nashville, Tennessee. The spirit of the young Black poets energized Gwendolyn. Soon after, she chose to have her work published by Broadside Press and later Third World Press, two Black-owned publishing companies. Gwendolyn wanted to help as much as she could to make these companies successful. It was important to her that

Black-owned companies publish books, too! *Aloneness* (1971) and *The Tiger Who Wore White Gloves* (1974) were two of her books for children published by Black presses.

In 1985, President Jimmy Carter gave Gwendolyn a special job. He asked her to become the Consultant in Poetry to the Library of Congress. She would write poems for special occasions, such as holidays. She was the first Black woman to have that job.

This honored poet has won awards from the American Academy of Arts and Letters, the Poetry Society of America, and the National Women's Hall of Fame. She was named the Poet Laureate for Illinois. Schools have been named in her honor. In Chicago, Illinois, Chicago State University created the Gwendolyn Brooks Center for African-American Literature and Culture.

Gwendolyn Brooks celebrated her eighty-third birthday in the year 2000. She is a professor of English at Chicago State University and continues to write poetry every day.

Virginia Hamilton
BORN **1936** - DIED **2002**

Distinguished Children's Author

Virginia Hamilton and her two sisters and two brothers stared wide-eyed as their mother told them a family story. The children never tired of listening to the grown-ups tell stories about their ancestors. Her mother recited:

> *As a young boy, your Grandpa Levi Perry and his mother escaped slavery through the Underground Railroad. He married and had ten children.*

I was one of those children. Your Grandpa worked hard. He bought a farm in Yellow Springs, Ohio. He always told his children stories about how he ran away from slavery. . . .

From listening to the stories in childhood, Virginia grew up to be the most famous storyteller of the Hamilton family.

Virginia was born on March 12, 1936, in Yellow Springs, Ohio. The Hamiltons lived on a 12-acre farm where they raised hogs and chickens. They grew corn, tomatoes, and cucumbers.

For Virginia and her siblings, life on the farm was wonderful. They played day and night. They jumped rope on the porch. They made their own stilts and balanced their small limbs on the high wooden legs. What fun they had!

Virginia loved to play, but she also loved to read and write. From the time she was in elementary school she wrote about all kinds of topics—from things about her life to things about outer space. Her teacher

*Virginia enjoyed playing on the family farm with her
brothers, sisters, and cousins.*

always loved reading the young girl's imaginative stories.

Once an author came to her class for a school visit. Virginia knew right away what she wanted to be. "I'm going to be a famous writer," the 11-year-old announced.

When Virginia graduated from Bryan High School in Yellow Springs, Ohio, she ranked at the top of her class. She won a scholarship to Antioch College, a small school that was just a mile away from home. Virginia liked Antioch, but she wanted to take more writing classes. So she transferred to Ohio State University in Columbus, Ohio. While there, she wrote many stories about unusual characters. "You're very talented," professors often told the young writer.

After Virginia graduated from Ohio State University in 1958, she packed her bags and moved to New York City. Her goal was to have a career as a writer.

Getting a job in New York as a writer was hard, so Virginia worked as a bookkeeper. She also sang in nightclubs. She met artists and musicians and writers. One

Virginia Hamilton at age five. Her first children's book was entitled Zeely.

of those writers was Arnold Adoff, a poet and teacher. He became her husband. They married on March 16, 1960. They had two children, Leigh and Jaime.

Even as she got older, Virginia dreamed of becoming a published writer. She sent her stories to one publisher, then another. They wrote back, "Sorry, we're not interested." Virginia was almost ready to give up.

Then a friend who was an editor gave her an idea. She reminded Virginia about a story she had written in school. Virginia looked for the story and sent it to her friend. That story became Virginia's first children's book, *Zeely*. The book is about a young girl who believes a neighbor's daughter is an African queen. The book was published in 1967.

Children loved her book. Adults did, too. Virginia's family was very proud of her. Virginia was happy that she had not given up.

Soon Virginia was typing away again. She wrote mysteries, ghost stories, and stories about strange characters. Virginia also liked writing about families and about the lives of important people in history, such as the actor Paul Robeson and the writer W. E. B. DuBois.

The Girl Who Spun Gold, *written by Virginia Hamilton and illustrated by Leo and Diane Dillon, is a magical African-American telling of the famous fairy tale* Rumpelstiltskin.

Virginia Hamilton lived and worked in Ohio. Her home was built on land that has been in her family for generations.

Over the years, Virginia received many awards and honors for her books. She won the John Newbery Medal for *M.C. Higgins, the Great* and the Coretta Scott King Award for *The People Could Fly: American Black Folktales*. Virginia received the American Library Association Best Book Award for *Cousins*. In 1992 she received the Hans Christian Andersen Medal for her lifetime contribution to children's literature. In 1995 she received the Laura Ingalls Wilder Award for her entire body of work. She was also the first writer for children to receive a John D. and Catherine T. MacArthur Fellowship.

Virginia Hamilton passed away on Tuesday, February 19, 2002.

Walter Dean Myers

BORN 1937

"Best Job in the World"

Walter Milton Myers was born in Martinsburg, West Virginia, less than seven miles from the plantation on which his family had been slaves. Walter's mother died when he was only three years old. His father was too poor to take care of Walter and his six brothers and sisters.

Florence and Herbert Dean were friends of the family. They offered to help by raising Walter and two of his sisters. The Deans lived in Harlem, a mostly Black community in New York City. Life in Harlem was very different for Walter than the life he had known in West Virginia but he loved the city and his new family. His new mother, Florence, taught Walter to read when he was four. Herbert, his father, told him great stories about ghosts and monsters.

Young Walter liked school, especially reading. But he wished the books he read in school had stories about his neighborhood, Harlem. He also wished some of the stories were about Black people.

Walter had another problem. He could not speak very well. Often teachers did not understand what he was trying to say. One

This picture of Walter was taken in 1945 when he was eight years old.

Walter grew up in Harlem.

day in class, Walter was asked to read aloud from a book of poems. When he did not speak clearly, his classmates pointed and laughed at him. Walter became angry and threw his book across the room. He was sent to the principal's office.

His teacher, Mrs. Conway, had an idea. She told the class to write their own poems. Walter wrote a poem using only words he could pronounce. When he read his poem to the class, he was praised. Writing his own poems and stories seemed like a good idea.

Walter enjoyed writing poems and, later, stories. Some of the stories he wrote were like the ones his father had told him. He also liked reading stories. Although he was praised for his poems and stories, he still did not do very well in school. Sometimes, instead of going to school, he would go to the park and read or write in his notebook.

When he was 14, he won a prize in a writing contest. He told his parents that he wanted to be a writer. His parents did not know of anyone who made a living writing stories and poems. "You need a good job," his

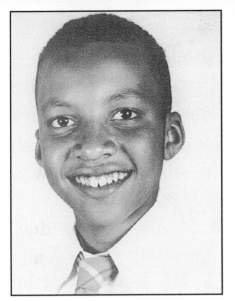

Walter used ideas from his childhood experiences in books he later wrote as an adult.

father said. "Perhaps you can work in the post office one day."

Walter, confused about what he wanted to do and what was available to Blacks, joined the army on his seventeenth birthday. His mother cried. His father was disappointed. They had both hoped he would continue his education.

Walter did not like army life. He trained to fight in war. He also played basketball for an army team. Years later he would use his army experiences to write *Fallen Angels*, a book about soldiers who fought in the Vietnam War.

When Walter finished his tour of duty in the army, he looked for a job in civilian life. He worked as a messenger, a factory worker, and then got a job in the post office. He didn't like these jobs and spent his spare time doing what he did love, writing.

In 1960, Walter began to send his stories to magazines and newspapers. Soon he was getting published. He wrote for the *National Enquirer, Negro Digest, The Delta Review,* and other publications. He also met other Black writers who encouraged him. The writers he met, John Killens, Langston Hughes, and James Baldwin, had already published books. They all encouraged him to continue writing.

Then in 1968, Walter's life changed. The Council on Interracial Children's Books was holding a contest for Black writers. Walter had never written a children's book. That didn't stop him, though. He wrote a short story about a group of kids who try to explain why the day ends. He called the story *Where Does the Day Go?*

The story won the contest! Walter was very happy. He was even happier when the story was made into a book in 1969. Then Walter got a job with a publishing company. His work involved helping new authors get their books published.

Even though Walter's job kept him busy, he never stopped writing. He published more short stories and two picture books, *The Dancers,* about a young boy who discovers ballet and *Fly, Jimmy, Fly,* about a young boy who wants to fly. To thank his foster parents for all the hard work they had done for him, he changed his name from Walter Milton Myers to Walter Dean Myers.

In 1977, Walter decided to spend all of his time writing. He wrote stories for newspapers and travel articles for magazines. His work took him to South America, Asia,

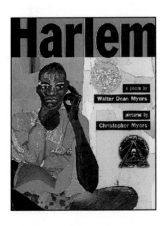

Walter has written many books about characters who live in Harlem.

and Africa. Then Walter met an editor who had read one of his short stories about Black teens in Harlem.

"Why don't you write about Harlem?" the editor asked. "Didn't you grow up there?"

Walter decided to write a story about growing up in Harlem and his friends there. He called the story *Fast Sam, Cool Clyde, and Stuff.*

In his books, Walter shares the everyday experiences of Black children and teens. He wants young people to be proud of their culture.

Walter Dean Myers has written more than 60 books for children and teenagers. Many of his books have won awards and honors. He has won the Coretta Scott King Award five times. Two of his books, *Somewhere in the Darkness* and *Scorpions,* have won Newbery Honors, and his book *Monster* was the first winner of the Michael L. Printz Award.

"I have the best job in the world," Walter says. "I get to do what I love best, writing."